XTREME ART

DRAW MANGA CHIBI!

CHRISTOPHER HART

WATSON-GUPTILL PUBLICATIONS/NEW YORK

INTRODUCTION

Chibi is a style of Japanese cartoons that is amazingly popular with kids all over the world. Chibi characters are short, round, and cute. But even though chibis are little, they have giant personalities! Chibis are hyper-adorable and irresistibly squeezable. Even chibi villains are cute. There are chibi people, pets, and monsters. Everyone loves chibis!

This book will help you draw all kinds of fun chibi characters. Each drawing is broken down into four simple steps. Start by tracing or drawing step 1. Then add the red lines in steps 2, 3, and 4. It's that easy!

You'll find a huge variety of chibi characters to draw, from wizards to ballerinas, from sword fighters to fairies. A few of the drawings have backgrounds, which you can either trace or draw if you like.

I believe that art should be fun. And nothing is more fun than drawing chibis. So get out your pencil and let's get started!

Tips for Using This Book

Trace or draw what you see in step 1. Then add the new lines (shown in red) in steps 2, 3, and 4. Draw with a light, sketchy line. Don't worry about getting it perfect on the first try.

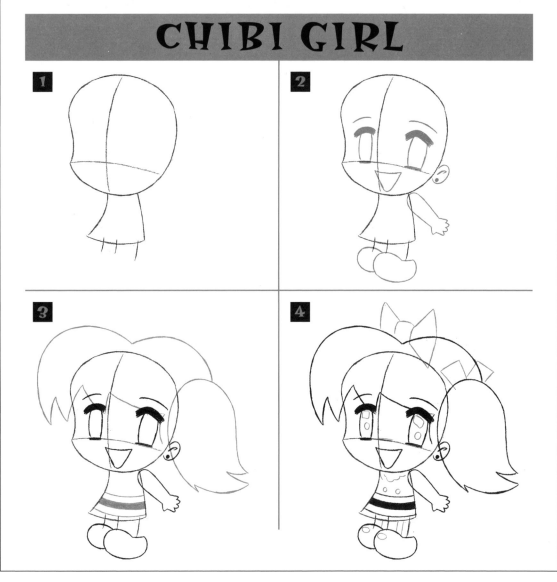

CHIBI GIRL

1

2

3

4

When you've finished the steps, erase the guidelines (the criss-crosses) and any other lines you don't want to keep. Go over the other lines to make them darker.

Color it in, and you've got a clean, bold drawing!

Let's start with some basics for drawing chibi-style characters.

Chibis are shorter, rounder, and cuter than other manga characters. To help show you the difference, I've drawn the same girl two different ways. Here she is drawn as a regular manga-style cartoon. Below, she's drawn as a chibi.

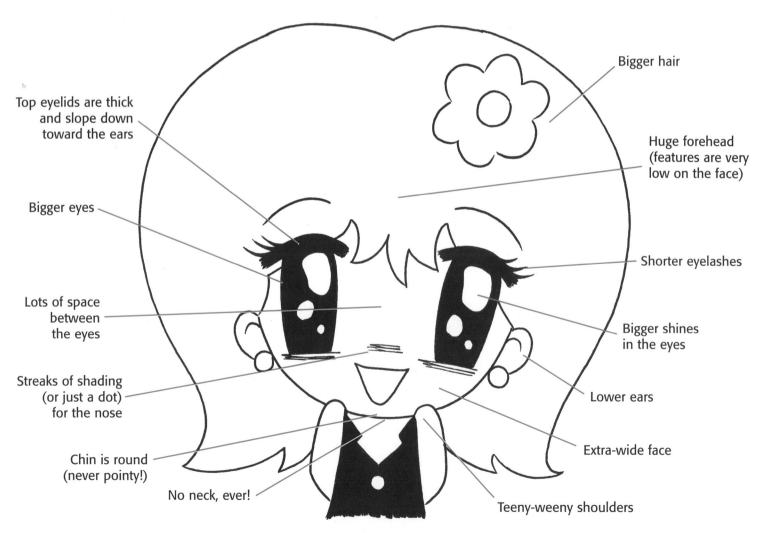

Bigger hair

Huge forehead (features are very low on the face)

Top eyelids are thick and slope down toward the ears

Bigger eyes

Shorter eyelashes

Lots of space between the eyes

Bigger shines in the eyes

Streaks of shading (or just a dot) for the nose

Lower ears

Extra-wide face

Chin is round (never pointy!)

No neck, ever!

Teeny-weeny shoulders

Chibis have eyes that are huge and full of shines. To draw them, start by drawing the overall shape of the eye. Then fill in the details. Just follow these steps and you'll see how simple and fun it is!

The eyelids should tilt down

1. DRAW "TALL" EYES.

2. MAKE THE TOP EYELIDS REALLY THICK.

The ends of the eyelids should have these points on them.

3. ADD EYELASHES TO THE ENDS, THEN DRAW TWO HUGE SHINES IN EACH EYE.

4. COLOR IT ALL IN (EXCEPT THE SHINES). ADD THE EYEBROWS.

Most real people are about six and a half heads tall. But chibis are only two heads tall. This means that a chibi's head is as big as its body! Chibi legs are short, while the legs of regular-sized characters are long. If you draw a chibi and it doesn't look cute enough, go back and check the proportions. Chances are, you need to make the head bigger.

Because chibis are so short and round, their bodies are easy to draw. The rule of thumb when drawing chibis is: Keep it simple. Look at the drawings below. You can see how their bodies are made up of basic shapes put together.

Here are a few popular ways to draw chibi hands and fingers.

Here are some more tips to help you.

Chibi bodies start off narrow but get wider toward the feet, which can be pretty big.

Keep it simple! Draw hands like this...

The arms get thinner as they travel toward the hands...

The fingers are tiny and delicate...

...not like this!

...not straight like this!

...not fat and chunky like this!

Chibi characters are small, but they usually have big feet. So how do you make small feet look big? You do it by making them short, chunky, and round. Look at the difference between regular cartoon feet and the chibi-style feet below.

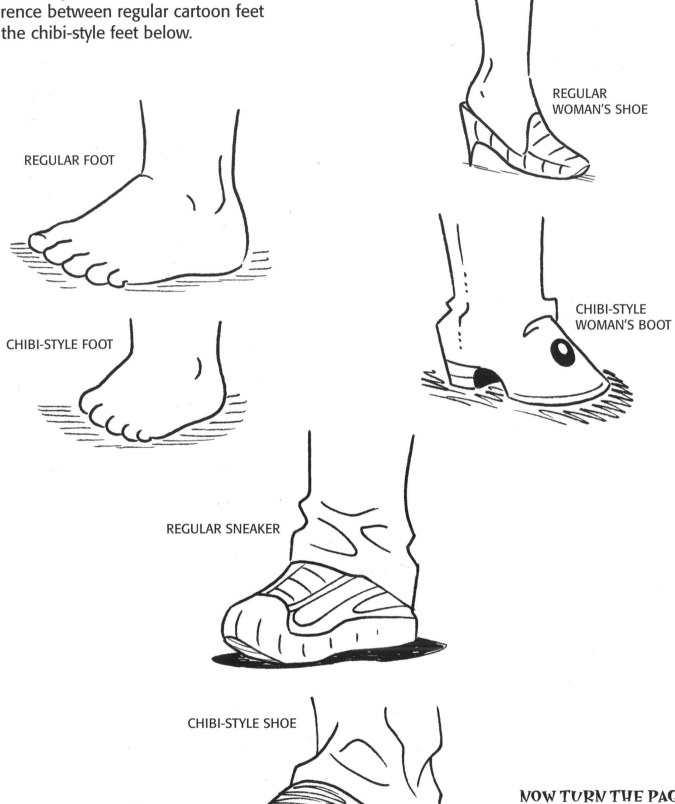

REGULAR WOMAN'S SHOE

REGULAR FOOT

CHIBI-STYLE WOMAN'S BOOT

CHIBI-STYLE FOOT

REGULAR SNEAKER

CHIBI-STYLE SHOE

NOW TURN THE PAGE AND START DRAWING CUTE MANGA CHIBIS!

BABY BUNNY

1

2

3

4

GOOFY GRIN

1

2

3

4

BULLY BOY

1

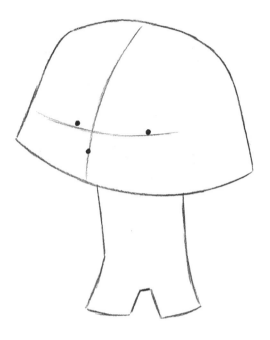

2

3

4

EXPLORER BOY

1

2

3

4

COCOA CAFÉ

1

2

3

4

MINI KNIGHT

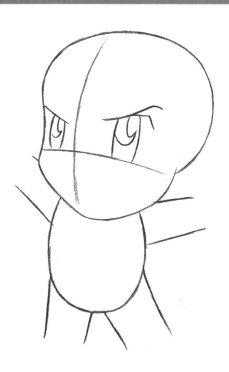

BALLET DANCER

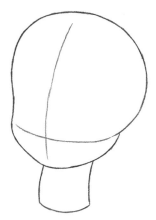

FIGHTING FURBALL

1

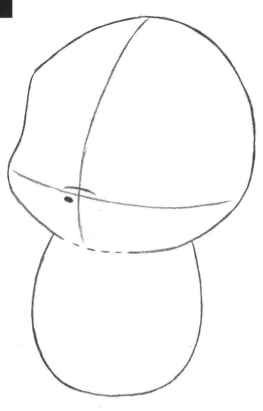

2

3

4

KITTY CRAZY

1

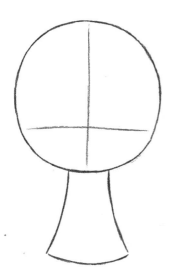

2

3

4

LASER LARRY

1

2

3

4

1

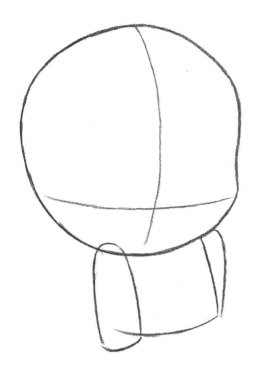

2

3

4

1

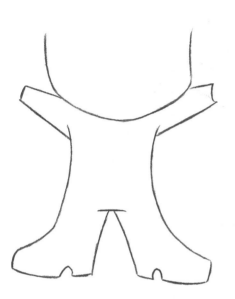

2

3

4

BATTLE PRINCESS

1

2

3

4

SUMO-SAMURAI

1

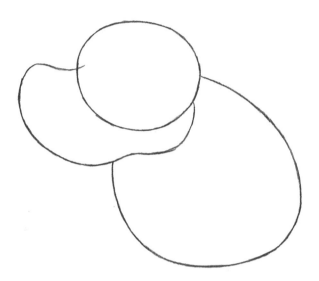

2

3

4

MAGIC EMPRESS

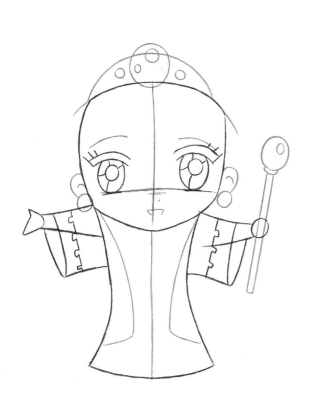

FRUSTRATED FREDDY

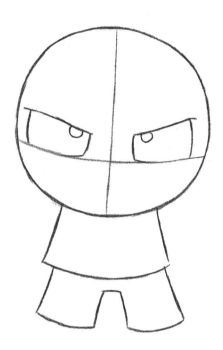

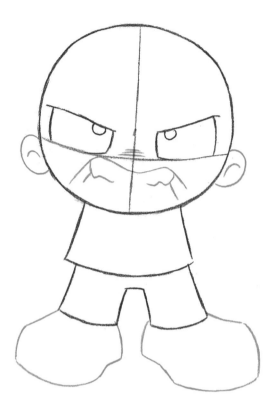

SNOWBALL FIGHT

1

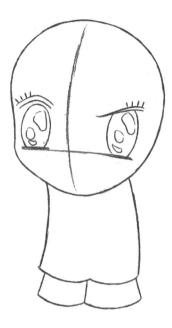

2

3

4

BIG IDEA

1
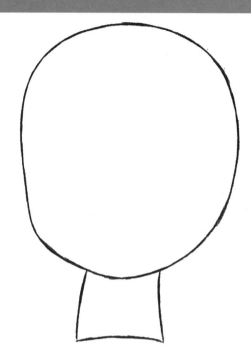

2

3

4

ROCKIN' GIRL

1

2

3

4

TRAINING KID

1

2

3

4

FURIOUS FAIRY

1

2

3

4

SURFIN' SALLY

1

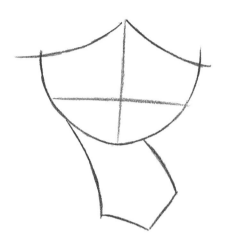

2

3

4

SURPRISED SERENA

1

2

3

4

ROCKET GIRL

PUPS & KISSES

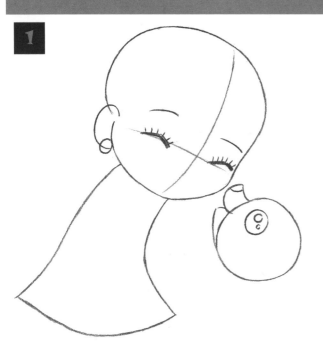

Senior Acquisitions Editor: Julie Mazur
Designer: Bob Fillie, Graphiti Design, Inc.
Production Manager: Hector Campbell
Text set in 13-pt Formata Regular

All drawings by Christopher Hart.

Cover art by Christopher Hart.
Text copyright © 2004 by Christopher Hart.
Illustrations copyright © 2004 by Christopher Hart.

First published in 2004 by
Watson-Guptill Publications,
Nielsen Business Media
a division of the Nielsen Company
770 Broadway, New York, NY 10003
www.Watsonguptill.com

Library of Congress Control Number: 2004108366

ISBN-13: 978-0-8230-0368-6
ISBN-10: 0-8230-0368-X

Printed in China

First printing, 2004

3 4 5 6 7 8 / 11 10 09 08 07